Home Communion

A Practical Guide

Carolyn Headley

Tutor in Liturgy and Spirituality, Wycliffe Hall, Oxford

GROVE BOOKS LIMITED
RIDLEY HALL RD CAMBRIDGE CB3 9HU

Contents

Acknowledgments

I would like to thank those who have encouraged the writing of this booklet, in particular the staff and students of Wycliffe Hall. I particularly thank those who have read the script and made helpful contributions: Colin Buchanan, Trevor Lloyd, Anne Barton, David Wenham, and Susan Barrington.

Further Resources

Wright, T, *Holy Communion for Amateurs* (Hodder Christian Books, 1999)

Culling, E, *Making the Most of Communion* (Grove Spirituality booklet S 66)

Autton, N, *Visiting the Sick: A Guide for the Laity* (London: Mowbray, 1980)

Dudley, M, *A Manual for Ministry to the Sick* (London: SPCK)

Botting, M, *Christian Healing in the Parish* (Grove Worship booklet W 42)

Headley, C, *The Laying on of Hands in the Parish Healing Ministry* (Grove Worship booklet W 104)

Church of England website: www.cofe.anglican.org/commonworship

Church House Publishing materials will include: Pastoral Services which includes Wholeness and Healing; Ministry to the Sick; and Holy Communion with the sick and housebound: Order One and Two (large print cards).

The Cover Illustration is by Valerie Turner

Copyright © Carolyn Headley 2000

First Impression April 2000
ISSN 0144-1728
ISBN 1 85174 429 0

1
Introduction

Holy Communion brings a tangible expression of the greatness and love of God and the transforming power of Christ into the centre of our life and situation. To administer communion is therefore a great privilege. Many are now able to share in this ministry as there is widespread authorization of lay people to distribute the bread and the wine. It is also generally understood that this authorization includes the highly responsible commission of taking the elements to the homes of those who are cut off from main church services. This practical guide to conducting home communions is aimed at facilitating this ministry.

There are many reasons why people are unable to be in church for a service. Sickness, whether acute and short-term or chronic and long-term, is the most obvious cause. There are also those who are basically well in themselves, but who have significant difficulty in getting to church. Physical disability, agoraphobia, conditions that require confinement to the home (such as need for oxygen or other machine support), unusual vulnerability to temperature, light or other environmental stress, or general debilitation through old age can all keep an otherwise well person at home. Carers and family are often unable to leave the person with the primary need and also appreciate ministry. Many of those to whom we minister will be in residential care, where we find ourselves also touching the lives of fellow residents and staff.

The year 2000 provides a timely occasion to review this ministry. This is the year when both the ASB communion rites and the *Ministry to the Sick* auxiliary rites officially lapse. They are superseded in December this year by the new texts which are authorized from Advent Sunday, 3rd December. These are Orders 1 and 2 of the Communion service in *Common Worship*, and the auxiliary provision in *Wholeness and Healing*, which will be included in the secondary volume *Pastoral Services*. All these are to be available also in *Visual Liturgy* and on the official Church of England web site. At the time of writing there is good hope that within the next few months the Bishop of Chelmsford's working party report on 'The Ministry of Healing' will also be published. It is into this situation that this booklet is directed. Its concern is not centrally textual, but the provision of new texts does give a good opportunity for re-thinking pastoral practice.

2

The Purpose of the Visit

i) The Meaning of Holy Communion

A Focus on Christ

Holy Communion is the act that Christ instituted, to be repeated by his followers, who thereby remember his life, death and resurrection, and through which they know his presence with them by his Holy Spirit. Through the simple sharing of bread and wine we are brought into a moment of true communion with the one who gave his life for us and whose blood was outpoured for us. As we recall the events we open our lives afresh to the living Lord who, in his love for us, comes to us by his Spirit that he may dwell in us and we in him.

This primary reason for the communion service is of great importance to those to whom we minister. To know the love of Christ in their lives, the power of his indwelling, and the reality of his life in them and theirs in him, brings a life-giving perspective to what is otherwise limited and bound by their physical restriction.

A Family Meal

Holy Communion is, by its very nature, a meal to be shared when believers gather together—a family meal. The family extends beyond the few participating in the home communion. All those who believe become the children of God, co-heirs of the kingdom, who call almighty God by the intimate name of 'Abba.' So when taking communion to those who are at home, the minister brings a reminder that they belong to this wider family, despite the physical isolation. This is best understood when backed up with expressions of love from that family.

A Healing Sacrament

The broken body of Christ on the cross sums up all the brokenness of humanity: spiritual, in sin; physical, in suffering and death; emotional, in the agony of dying and the pain of watching the suffering of those who loved him; psychological, in the cry of desolation from the cross; social, in the rejection it epitomized and the running away of the disciples. In the resurrection and ascension we see the transforming of the human condition in Christ: sin is forgiven; his broken body is raised from the dead; he is restored to the right hand of the Father; he invites his disciples to be with him in glory; and he meets with them and makes himself known to them. All the destructive forces of sin and death are transformed into a pathway of healing and life. Such is the message of the communion service. In our brokenness we can come to the one was broken for us and is now raised from the dead, who offers us the path of life and the promise of our ultimate healing in eternal life in the presence of God.

A Feast of Hope

At the Last Supper Jesus looked forwards to a future time when he would drink the fruit of the vine 'new with you in my Father's kingdom' (Matt 26.29; compare Mark 14.25, Luke 22.16, 18). And in 1 Cor 11.26 the Corinthians are told 'every time you eat this bread and drink the cup, you proclaim the Lord's death until he comes.' So there is a future component to the communion which sets us looking towards the coming of the kingdom and the second coming of the Lord. For many of those to whom we minister at home this future aspect will be preparing them for their own death. It is an offer of hope and life, which transforms the worldly view that death is the end. With this hope as part of the service the temporal boundary of expected life is challenged.

Christ's Presence Recognized

All these aspects of a communion service contribute towards a fresh realization that Christ is present. Some live daily with an assurance that Christ is with them, but for others the insidious depression and isolation of loneliness makes them less certain. Communion is a true life-line for many people with the presence of Christ becoming a tangible reality.

ii) Being Part of the Church, the Body of Christ

Holy Communion is essentially a corporate act, by the people of God, gathered together round his table. However, there has been a practice of taking communion to those unable to attend a central gathering from as early as AD 150, if not before. Justin Martyr, in Rome, records how it was taken to such people by deacons. There is a principle of inclusion in the body of Christ, through the sharing of the bread and wine, even if separated by physical distance. Where significant hindrance prevents a person joining others in Holy Communion, it is the church that goes to them with the tangible signs of belonging to the body, and the opportunity to partake of the body.

This clearly rules out the taking of communion to individuals who *are* able to join the wider fellowship. This is not a home-order facility. Those who can be with the gathered church should be there.

iii) Bringing a Sense of Value

Each individual person is of value in God's eyes. This basic and somewhat obvious premise is not always the experience of those coping with disability, or facing sickness, or loneliness, or feeling trapped in a caring role. Without a daily rhythm of outside interests and activities, work, or a full active existence, days can become very empty and long. When no-one visits, it is possible to feel that you are of no value and no importance. If visitors do come they can often be coming on their own terms—when convenient to them, time conscious with their programme, and sure of their own agenda in the visit. This can also be accompanied by a patronizing attitude, making the person feel lucky to have been given the time and now in the debt of the visitor. The possibility of feeling that God does not care either is very high. How can we avoid such dangers?

Understanding the people we visit will help. This means that the communion minister will start where the communicants are, talking to them, getting to know their past story and what has brought them to this point in life. It means listening to what they think of their situation and how they perceive themselves. No assumptions should be made in this process. Neither can assumptions be made about their faith, their spiritual journey, or their day-to-day relationship with God. Having done that, the minister needs to be mindful that their present state is set in the context of their whole life. They have a past with all its richness, a present which will have many different facets for them, and a future which holds all kinds of hopes and fears.

Many aspects of life will be altered by being housebound, whatever the cause. The communicant may be going through the initial implications of various changes, or be quite used to living with the situation. There may be emotional and psychological adjustments as the body no longer responds to the inner expectations. Friendships can be interrupted as shared activities are no longer possible. Family relationships are changed as the usual pattern of meeting or visiting has to change. Reading, cooking one's favourite meal, or going down to the pub—all the 'normal' relaxations and activities—may have to be re-negotiated. Carers may have totally altered their lives, too, to be able to devote time, energy, and resources towards looking after their relative or friend.

How all this feels inside will vary from person to person, and how long it takes to come to terms with such changes, if that happens at all, will also vary. The reaction may include pain or possibly anger. A process of bereavement may be in evidence, because of losing the hopes and promises of the future as they had been envisaged. Communicants may feel inhibited in expressing their feelings, mindful that others often turn negative with someone who is seen as 'moaning' or 'sorry for themselves.' When communion is brought to them, it is a reminder of the presence of Christ who accepts them as they are, and knows and understands their inner pain and turmoil. As ministers in this situation, it is our privilege to allow an openness, meet them where they are, and see them as whole people, with all the richness and fullness that is their identity, and all the hidden pain that is a daily reality for them. In accepting them we give them permission to acknowledge and express their whole experience, and we value them for who they are.

3
Who Should Go?

i) Authorized Lay Ministers of Communion

Most mainstream denominations now authorize lay people to administer Holy Communion. In the Church of England this requires authorization by the bishop, although Readers are automatically licensed to distribute communion. For services at home, lay ministers of communion will take elements that have already been consecrated, either straight from a church service, or from a place of safe keeping. The service wording will reflect this, as a lay person will not use the consecration prayer but an authorized reference to the occasion on which the bread and wine were consecrated.

The advantages of lay ministry in this area are significant. The sense of inclusion in the body of Christ is enhanced for the communicant by receiving ministry from other members of the congregation. Where this happens immediately after a service there is the added sense of belonging that comes from knowing that you have just been prayed for, and sometimes from the fact that the service has not even finished. The opportunity to foster this ministry among those who have clear pastoral gifts can bring much blessing to the recipients. There is also the added advantage of being able to use those who have time, and the willingness to give it generously, to those they visit. If this is coupled with other regular visits, then an established relationship will make the communion a richer experience for both the minister and the communicant..

ii) The Clergy

There still remains, for some parishioners, a sense that communion is the proper business of the clergy. If offering lay ministry leads to a sense of being rejected or marginalized even further on the part of the communicant, then clearly the clergy should make every effort to minister at least occasionally.

iii) Representatives of the Church Family

Gathering a few people together for a small home communion service may be appreciated if the communicant is a member of a home group, or is a PCC member, or has a few friends in the congregation who would like to pray with him or her.

iv) Carers and Family

Others who are present in the house or residential home can be invited to share in the communion service. This is often an important and meaningful occasion. However, some prefer to be on their own , especially if they want to confide in the minister, or to share inner fears for prayer.

v) Common Misgivings

The ministry of taking communion to someone at home can raise some anxiety, especially for those who have never taken services of any kind.

Perhaps the most common is an acute sense of inadequacy, and concern at being thought to be acting 'above one's station,' to use an outdated but meaningful expression. As the ministry of the sacrament has been the exclusive domain of ordained priests there can be a sense of inferiority. Whilst genuine, these misgivings are based on some false premises. All Christians are called to minister in their baptism. The call and the form of ministry are different, but should not be seen as being superior or inferior. There is privilege in all ministry, but this comes from sharing in the work of Christ and being used to bring a sense of his presence into a situation. The privilege is not one of position or status. Consequently the lay communion minister, who is called to the ministry to share in the work of Christ's church, and is authorized by the bishop, has the full sanction of the church to be carrying out this ministry.

Sometimes the sense of inadequacy can come from thinking one must be particularly 'holy' to be handling the things of God in giving communion. No-one's credentials to minister are based on levels of goodness—it would rule out too many of us! We are all called to be earthen vessels, humble in our recognition of our weakness, and our need for the power and love of God to equip us for the task to which he calls us. A prayerful attitude, and time spent in preparation for this ministry, will help us to be open to the sense of Christ at work in us and through us, for the good of those to whom we minister.

There can also be anxiety about being accepted. For some communicants there is an established assumption that only the priest is acceptable. It can take time, understanding, patience and careful building of relationships to overcome the reliance on the traditional pattern of ministry. Much of this will involve assurance that the recipient is not being passed over or abandoned by the parish clergy. Some sort of pattern of attendance could help with this, such as monthly communion by the ordained, and more regular visits of communion brought from Sunday services by a lay minister. Distinguishing between traditional expectations and personal rejection is necessary to avoid hurt and loss of self-confidence in the lay communion ministers.

For all ministers there can be a misgiving about entering into another person's home and private and personal space. Although there by invitation it is a healthy thing to remember whose home this is, and to be respectful of boundaries. The boundary of privacy means not being nosey. Respecting space and independence means not interfering in the way people choose to live, not trying to organize them or make decisions for them. Over time a relationship of trust will grow, but no assumptions should be made which pre-empt what can be quite a long process for some people.

4

The Service

i) How Often and How Long?

Getting a good pattern of home communions is important. Regular communions that are arranged too frequently can lead to letting down the communicant in busy periods. This can hurt deeply, as the expected communion can be a real highpoint, which is eagerly anticipated, and therefore all the more important. Letting someone down can increase their sense of low value and marginalization. Home communions need to be given high priority once arranged.

Working out a suitable pattern needs to be done individually, as some will feel a need for communion more frequently than others.

A communion visit will normally include some time to talk in order to see how things are going, asking for prayer needs, giving some news and prayer needs of others, explaining the service (if necessary), and the service itself. Beyond this the length of a communion visit will vary. Those who are relatively well but housebound will find a fleeting visit difficult. Careful handling of their sensitivity in this area is necessary. Giving some indication as to how long you are coming for when arranging the visit will help the communicant to cope with your leaving. It may be helpful to leave them soon after the communion, so that they can reflect on their time with God, ponder the reading, pray further and slowly adjust to their normal life and routine. Jumping up to get a cup of tea and begin to chit-chat can deny the work of the Holy Spirit in their post-communion reflection. If they are anticipating a longer visit then their deflated expectations can be painful—and who will eat the fish-paste sandwiches that are waiting in the next room, if you leave without accepting their intended invitation to tea? A good compromise may be to make a distinction between a social visit, with a cup of tea and a chat, and a home communion visit, which will be more focussed and probably shorter.

In either case the quality of time you spend with a person is more important than the amount. Someone who does not stop to take off their coat, who is looking at their watch every few moments, and sending out body language of haste and impatience, could be less helpful in forty minutes than someone who gives total attention and loving care for twenty. Arranging one's watch before arriving, or sitting within an easy glance of a clock, so that reference to either is minimal, will help the busy minister.

People who are very ill can rarely concentrate for long. They find it incredibly tiring to make conversation, and need rest to recover. So do not stay longer than is necessary. More frequent short visits are more helpful than longer less frequent ones. So someone who is more unwell will probably not be able to manage more than a short service. For them the priority will be for you to enter into their situation quickly, sensitively and with ease, and leave afterwards quietly and without delaying, demanding the minimum effort on their part.

ii) Prayer and Preparation

Prayer is foundational to the ministry—prayer on a regular basis as the minister's relationship with God grows and develops, prayer specifically for the person to whom communion is taken, asking for guidance in appropriate readings, prayers, and approach to their needs, and prayer immediately prior to going, in order to focus on Christ and be open to his leading and guidance through the Holy Spirit.

In addition to prayer the minister needs to prepare practically. Arrival at the home needs to be as purposeful and calm as possible, enabling the communicant to concentrate on God and his presence, rather than on practical preparations. This will entail making all the choices regarding material and content prior to going, and carefully ensuring you have everything necessary for the service (see the section on 'Practicalities').

In order to arrive with a quiet and prayerful attitude, the minister will need to allow plenty of time for the journey. Try to make this a journey dedicated to this purpose, rather than tacking it on to the end of a busy and unpredictable day. Whilst wanting to make good use of time, there is a danger in arranging too many home communions in succession. It can lead to a sense of being rushed and make it difficult to alter the schedule for unexpected but necessary ministry. If taking elements that have already been consecrated, there should be additional care in preparation and respect for the ministry being undertaken. For example, taking the bread and wine on a trip to the supermarket in your pocket is not appropriate!

iii) Preparation by the Communicant

Those who are to receive communion should be encouraged to prepare themselves. The underlying state of health will affect this, but as many who receive home communion are basically well, although physically limited, a certain amount of preparation may be possible. You could encourage the use of one or two prayers earlier in the day. This could include some of the collects, prayers from the authorized provision for services of *Wholeness and Healing*, and an encouragement to review their life before God in preparation for confession and receiving communion. Having a selection of suitable prayers and readings printed out for the use of communicants is useful (copyright considerations allowing), or encouraging them to have their own prayer book or service book.

Reading a pre-agreed passage from the Bible, or the readings used in the service from which the elements are being brought, or encouraging use of a devotional book can be helpful. This is especially enriching if the communion minister also reads the same to enable shared reflection. If communion is being taken immediately after the Sunday morning service, it may be helpful to suggest that communicants watch a televised service or listen to a service on the radio as part of their preparation.

Getting the room or table ready may be a way for the communicant to prepare spiritually, if physical strength permits. Some people like to keep a particular cloth, candle, picture or cross to use when communion is brought.

iv) Forms of Service

The Common Worship services for *Wholeness and Healing* offer modern and traditional language forms for Holy Communion, after Order 1 and Order 2. The introductory notes make it clear that the service can be modified according to pastoral need and context.

The service can be a full service of Holy Communion, with an ordained minister presiding in the presence of the communicant, or a communion minister can take elements that are already consecrated. In the first case an authorized Eucharistic Prayer must be used. In the second case there are set words of introduction which make the connection with the celebration of Holy Communion by the wider church community.

'The Church of God, of which we are members, has taken bread and wine and given thanks over them according to our Lord's command. These holy gifts are now offered to us that, with faith and thanksgiving, we may share in the communion of the body and blood of Christ.'

The choice of which service to use as the basis for the communion will depend on the age and church experience of communicants, their state of health and the appropriate length for the service. There may also be expectations of the incumbent and PCC to take into account. Generally, older church members are still more comfortable with BCP or traditional language than with modern language services. However, the *Book of Common Prayer* itself is difficult to handle in a home communion, because of the page turning required. The Common Worship services in traditional language may be helpful here. The services in *Ministry to the Sick* contain a helpful range of alternatives: *The Celebration of Holy Communion with the Sick and Housebound* in modern and traditional language and orders for *The Distribution of Holy Communion to the Sick and Housebound*. Card versions of simplified services will be available and are easy to handle. A church may produce its own within the current guidelines. If the church has its own service booklets for normal use, then using these can be a point of continuity with the wider worshipping community.

A point to note, whatever the content, is that familiar words are often more helpful when someone is ill, or is already feeling cut off from what is known and loved. Consequently a home communion service is more helpfully shortened by having a few familiar prayers, and sections of the usual communion service, rather than by being too creative and introducing a lot of new material.

v) Sample orders of service

A Shortened Form for Home Communion *(following Order 1)*

The Greeting—which may include the Peace
Words of Introduction—if using consecrated elements
(The Collect for Purity)
Prayers of Penitence—either here or with the prayers of intercession
The Collect
Reading(s)
Intercessions, to include the Lord's Prayer if using consecrated elements
(Laying on of hands and anointing)
The Peace—this can be exchanged here or at the start of the service
Preparation of the table—final preparation of bread and wine
* The Eucharistic Prayer—unless using consecrated elements
* The Lord's Prayer
* Breaking of the Bread
  Invitation to Communion
  (Prayer of Humble Access)
  Giving of Communion
  Post-communion prayer
  The Grace or a blessing

The service notes say that the minister is free to modify or shorten given forms, according to pastoral need and context. However, those sections marked with an asterisk* are always used when an ordained minister is presiding. The sections in brackets ( ) are those considered non-essential.

The minimum required for a very sick person is as follows:

A Greeting—including the Peace
The Words of Introduction—if using consecrated elements
Prayers of Penitence
The Eucharistic Prayer—unless using consecrated elements
The Lord's Prayer
Reception (if able)
Post-communion prayer

vi) The Service in Detail

The Greeting: A liturgical greeting, such as *The Lord be with you*, with its reply, *And also with you*, or *Peace to this house and all who live in it*, with its reply, *The peace of the Lord be always with you*, gives the service a clear beginning.

Words of Introduction: If elements are being used that have been consecrated on another occasion, then the authorized words of introduction are inserted here. This sets the service in the context of the ongoing life of the church, and links the communion of the recipient to the celebration of communion by the wider church community.

The Collect for Purity: This prayer, which begins '*Almighty God, to whom all hearts are open...*' is well known, so it will easily come to mind in regular communicants. An alternative collect, in the services for *Wholeness and Healing*, is based on Jesus, the anointed Son of the Father, with the Holy Spirit bringing the blessings of the kingdom.

Prayers of Penitence: Here there is opportunity for a very personal and open form of ministry, in the privacy of one's own home. The use of silent reflection in review of life, and the opportunity to say a personal prayer of confession, may be helpful (either silently or out loud). Where this is done with a lay minister the appropriate format would be to offer a prayer for forgiveness afterwards, using the *us* form of words, rather than pronouncing an absolution with the *you* form. The *Book of Common Prayer* service of 'Order for the Visitation of the Sick,' majors on this aspect of ministry. It highlights the need that many have to feel free of their past sins, and the weight of conscience that these can bring, especially if their illness or old age is reminding them of their mortality. *Wholeness and Healing* offers a particularly appropriate invitation to confession. Although there are several forms of authorized prayers available, it is not necessary to use these. Suitable alternatives are allowed. It may be necessary for a lay minister to refer further ministry in this area to ordained clergy, if there is need for formal confession and absolution. The Prayers of Penitence can be used as part of the prayers of intercession.

The Collect: This is normally the collect of the week

Reading(s): If home communion is a regular ministry then use of the set readings for the previous Sunday can be a helpful reminder of the ongoing life of the church, of which the communicant is part. Always hearing readings related to sickness can reinforce a sense of hopelessness or introspection. An introduction such as 'Jane's daughter read this reading on Sunday,' or something which makes the communicant feel part of the church family, can be helpful and more personal.

Where the communicant is more acutely ill the need for more specific readings arises. *Wholeness and Healing* has a selection of readings and prayers. There are also commercial publications that are very helpful, offering handy books of resources that can easily be taken to a home communion situation (see the resources section on page 2).

A short thought: Some words based on the reading will underline it and give something to ponder. In some churches the sermon is taped, and where this happens a copy could be left with the communicant. Perhaps a summary of the sermon could be given. Similarly the news sheet, if it contains the readings and sermon points, could be left for further reflection. In such ways the minister can help the person to look at God's word and then look onwards in life, rather than just inwards to personal pain, difficulty, or loneliness.

It is important to think of the overall spiritual needs of those visited. How are they growing in their relationship with God? What challenge or inspiration or growth point will the reading bring for them?

Intercessions: It is necessary to distinguish between ongoing, long-term ministry and acute illness. In long-term ministry it helps to prompt concern for others, as well as concentrating on personal needs. It is also appropriate to ask if you could pray for parish needs or other sick or housebound people, or something that the communicant may have seen on television, such as an earthquake or famine or plane crash. Where prayer requests are listed on a news sheet that helps as a reminder. In acute situations it may not be as appropriate to pray for others, but is often still helpful. The Prayers of Penitence may form part of this time of intercession.

The laying on of hands and anointing with oil: If either or both of these are being used this ministry normally takes place after the Ministry of the Word, as part of the intercessions. Such ministry could take the form of holding a hand during a simple prayer for healing, or it can be a more formal ministry. The Common Worship services for *Wholeness and Healing* include forms and words for the Laying on of Hands and for Anointing. There are notes on their use, and a form of prayer to use with oil if not using that consecrated by the bishop of the diocese. If other members of the congregation or the family are present they can join in the ministry of the laying on of hands with the minister. An ordained minister should normally be responsible for the ministry of anointing. The Prayers of Penitence can be included at this point, if not used earlier in the service. (Other Grove booklets deal with prayer and ministry for healing at greater length).

The Peace: This can be exchanged either here or at the initial greeting at the start of the service.

Preparation of the table: Uncovering the bread, or pouring the wine from the cruet into the chalice, is done at this point if it has not been done before the service began. A prayer is provided for this moment in *Wholeness and Healing*.

The Eucharistic Prayer: If using a Eucharistic Prayer, one of the shorter authorized forms would be appropriate, choosing from the normal eucharistic provision of Common Worship services.

The Lord's Prayer: It is important that this is used in any service of Holy Communion, and is in a form that is familiar and enables full participation if at all possible. It is to be used as part of the intercessions when using *The*

Distribution of Holy Communion to the Sick and Housebound.

Breaking of the Bread: if an ordained minister is presiding in the presence of the sick person, then the breaking of the bread comes at this point.

Invitation to Communion: One of the familiar invitations may be used, or a suitable alternative. For example *Jesus is the Lamb of God who takes away the sin of the world. Blessed are those who are called to his supper,* with its reply, *Lord, I am not worthy to receive you, but only say the word and I shall be healed.*

Prayer of Humble Access: In this position the prayer relates to preparation for reception, but it can also be said earlier, following on from the ministry of intercession.

Giving of Communion: This is a prayerful, quiet and moving moment for most people. The minimum of movement, and time for quiet reflection afterwards, are appreciated. The communion is preferably given in both kinds, although it is often given in bread only. When a communicant is unable to take solid food it can be given in wine only. Those unable to receive at all should be assured that they are able to partake by faith in the body and blood of Christ, and to receive all his benefits.

A post-communion prayer: This can be free prayer, although most regular communicants would wish to join in a known post-communion prayer, or the Gloria, or the General Thanksgiving.

Blessing: Lay ministers of communion may say a prayer of blessing in the *us* form, or the Grace.

5

Practicalities

i) Setting out

Containers: The bread and wine, and oil if being used, should be transported in appropriate containers, which will not cause offence to the person receiving them, and which show some respect for the purpose for which they are being used. Whilst there is no necessity for using silver or glass containers, they are traditional and aesthetically appropriate. However, any suitable containers may be used.

The traditional vessels used for communion are as follows:

- The bread is carried in a *pyx*, a small box, usually silver, which sometimes has its own protective pouch with a cord on it so that it can be hung round the neck.
- The wine is carried in a *cruet*, a small bottle with a screw top, usually glass or silver. (If water is taken a second cruet is used).
- The oil is put in an *oil stock*, which is a small screw-top jar. Putting cotton wool inside this, soaked with oil, is easier to manage, as oil runs very freely and can be messy.
- For administration a small *paten* (the plate) and *chalice* (the cup) are used.
- A *spoon* is used for giving wine to someone too ill to handle a chalice.
- You may also want to take a small *cross*.

Home communion sets of varying sizes are available, with only the larger sets having all these items.

Using elements already consecrated: Whether taking the elements from a service, or from a place of safe-keeping, the ministry to the person being visited begins with collecting what is needed and departing. Whilst being aware of the dangers of investing a superstitious importance in how the elements are handled, it should be remembered that these things have been set aside with prayer for a particular and holy purpose. They become for us the body and blood of Christ by faith with thanksgiving. A prayerful attitude is therefore helpful and appropriate from collecting them to giving them in communion.

After a church service: The authorized communion ministers can be given the elements either at the distribution, or just before the dismissal, or after the service. A public prayer for those taking the communion, and those who will receive it, is a good way of making the link between those partaking who are present and those who are absent. It forms part of our intercession for those who are in need, and reminds the community of those who are unable to attend. This can be an extemporary prayer.

From a place of safe-keeping: A private prayer of commitment to the task, and intercession for the person who will receive, is a helpful way of preparing for this ministry. Whilst not a public prayer it nevertheless ensures a sense of continuity between the service in which the elements were set apart and the person to whom they are taken. (In some churches the consecrated elements will be kept in an 'aumbry,' and are referred to as 'reserved sacrament.')

Special requirements for some communicants: Bread: Those who have coeliac disease will need gluten-free bread. They can either provide their own at the time, if a full communion service is being used, or can provide it in advance for pre-consecrated bread to be available to an authorized communion minister. Gluten-free wafers can be purchased from ecclesiastical suppliers.

Wine: Whilst the church requires wine to be used for the communion, it may be necessary in some circumstances to use non-alcoholic grape juice. One obvious situation is taking communion to someone battling against alcoholism. However, there may also be medical considerations in other cases.

ii) Arriving and Greeting

From what has already been said, it follows that the arrival should be pre-arranged, on time, unhurried, and efficient. For the protection of communicants and for their peace of mind some recognizable form of identification is useful if the minister is not already known.

All the focus should be on the spiritual encounter for the communicant with God, rather than on the minister's busyness or problems! The extent of the greeting will vary, but basically should on this occasion be focussed on preparing for communion, listening to the communicants' perception of where they are and their concerns, rather than a general social visit.

iii) Preparing the Room

The chairs need to be close enough for a friendly atmosphere, for ease of helping the communicant with the service card, or for moving easily to lay on hands and give the communion without the distraction of scrambling over furniture or across a room. If preferred the minister may stand, although this can feel intimidating to the communicant.

There is usually a small table, or bedside table, that could be used for the communion, and this may require clearing off, removing ashtrays or other objects which might detract from the focus of the service. It is less usual to be able to rely on provision of a white cloth, so this should be taken. Laying out the elements before starting prevents distraction later on, and also helps the communicant to focus their thoughts. The emphasis should always be on helping the communicant to pray with ease, so anything that could be a distraction or an irritant should be avoided.

iv) Laying up the Table

- A white cloth *(that goes under all the things being used for the communion);*
- The bread, usually in the pyx or put on the paten;
- The wine in a small chalice, if it is being used;
- A purificator *(a small linen square or paper napkin to wipe the chalice after use);*
- An oil stock *(and an extra purificator or tissue, if oil is being used);*
- A small cross *(if desired);*
- A candle *(if desired);*
- A small spoon *(if someone is too ill to be able to drink out of a chalice);*
- Water *(some priests, doing a full communion service, may wish to add a little water to the wine, and/or to wash the fingers symbolically before the Eucharistic Prayer).*

Quietly chatting while all is prepared, and gradually changing the mood to one of reflection, helps ease into the service. There can sometimes be an awkwardness for people if they are not used to being ministered to at home, in the same way as one can feel slightly intimidated by a home visit from a doctor. Putting people at their ease is important. A simple explanation of the service is helpful for most people, as well as asking about preferences with regard to praying for them, or for how they would like to pray for others.

v) Receiving the Elements

For most people the way they receive will be same as in church. For the bread this will be with hands cupped, or onto the tongue for those with more high-church backgrounds. If wine is used it will normally be sipped from the chalice, although those from high-church backgrounds may not wish to touch the cup themselves.

Intinction may be used. This is when the bread, or wafer, is just dipped into the wine and placed on the tongue. This is less practical when using fresh bread, unless it is of a particularly solid kind, as it can disintegrate too quickly to get from cup to mouth. It is worth checking this out beforehand, with some of the bread you intend to use. Intinction is normally used when there is concern about passing germs or communicable diseases by use of a common cup. If a drop of wine is put on the bread beforehand, and allowed to dry, the alcohol will evaporate and it can then be a way for recovering alcoholics to receive both elements.

Those who are very ill may be unable to take bread and wine, as swallowing may be difficult or not allowed for medical reasons. In this case the merest crumb of wafer can be placed on the tongue, or drop of wine put on the tongue with a small spoon. Those who cannot manage even this small gesture need to be assured that they are receiving by faith.

6
Pastoral Considerations

i) What it is Like to Receive Communion at Home

The experience of receiving communion at home is not likely to be the same for any two people. However, some common reactions are as follows:

Gratitude: Many people are very grateful when someone takes the time and trouble to visit and especially to bring communion. However, whilst often being genuinely thankful for what they have received, it is all too easy to feel obliged to be grateful, and in some way to be in debt to the visitor.

Embarrassment: Having someone from the church in your home can be embarrassing. It is possible to feel under scrutiny or judgment—at the state of the house, at the relative poverty or wealth it demonstrates, and at what it reveals about you. It is also common for those who are sick to be in bed, or at least in nightclothes or lounge clothes, which can make them feel vulnerable and embarrassed. Illness can also produce embarrassing symptoms such as wind or smell, and this can be difficult for the communicant and the visitor. (As a tip, you may find breathing through your mouth enables you to cope better with unpleasant odours, and you are less likely to wrinkle your nose and show your discomfort).

Self-awareness: Being the focus of attention can be difficult for some people, especially if they normally prefer to be in the background. They may initially not be very at ease with the whole situation revolving around them and their needs.

Feeling special: The experience can be a very profound one in which the person is aware of being cared for, loved, and valued—both by the church and by God. It can sometimes produce strong emotions and a significant spiritual experience. Drawing alongside at such times is a real privilege.

Uncertainty: For many people it will be a new experience to receive communion individually, rather than as part of a big congregation. They may be uncertain of what will take place, what they should or should not do, whether they will 'get it right,' whether they should have confessed so much or should have said more about what they are facing. Such thoughts can jostle for attention before, during, and after the visit. Over time these will be addressed if home communion is repeated, but it is as well to be aware of the likely turmoil at first.

Spiritually disoriented: Simply being ill can affect the way a person is feeling, whether they can pray, or how they think and feel about God at all. This may be of concern to communicants, or they may not be aware of how different things are for them spiritually.

ii) Projection

It is worth remembering that communion ministers carry an identity with the organization, as well as being seen in their own right. This can be very positive as it gives the message that the wider church cares about the communicant, and that the body of Christ (and therefore Christ himself) loves them. However, it can conversely mean that negative feelings, hurts, and reactions can be projected onto the minister as well. Anger at God, anger at past wrongs by the church or confusion as to why they are suffering can all be projected. Taking this projection, whether comfortable or not, needs to be recognized for what it is. It should neither be allowed to puff up self importance and self gratification if it is praise and gratitude, or, just as likely, cause a sense of personal rejection or lead to taking umbrage when negative feelings are released. Getting into a situation of self-justification or counter-argument is to miss the point and risks doing further harm.

iii) Developing Ministries

There is a tendency to collude with the sense of uselessness or finality about being housebound. Helping such people to continue developing as individuals and in their spiritual life is important. This can include discovering new ways of ministry. For example, they may be able to pray on a regular basis for an aspect of the church's life. If this is linked to visits by those for whom they pray, then it also links them to the real world (for example, prayer for the Sunday children's groups, with visits from leaders and children). They could undertake to pray for particular individuals, giving a reciprocal ministry – being visited by the person for whom they are praying. They could talk to church members to help them to know what it is like to be housebound, so that more informed and sensitive ministry can develop. (This could be done by a taped interview, or by a few people visiting for this purpose). They could help the young to understand local history by speaking of their past. They could help someone learn to pray, sharing their knowledge and love of God. Enabling a person to give as well as receive can be a means of real blessing.

iv) Home Communion in a Home for the Elderly
Protocol

Carers need to know who is in the home, for security, and they need to protect the resident from visits when they would be too stressful, when the resident is too ill, or when they may need to do a procedure for the resident. So checking whether it is convenient to visit is important—even though your time may be limited as well! Some homes have an appointed chaplain. But chaplains are usually only too pleased when local clergy and church members visit and share the care. Liaising with them is important especially in terms of sacramental provision. They also like to know if someone is being visited regularly—and is therefore being 'looked after.'

Location

If the staff know when you are coming, they are usually able to work around the normal routine and allow you to meet in a resident's own room or a side room. It is difficult giving communion to one person in a home's day room, and it can take a long time to get a resident back to his or her room and settled. Sometimes you may be asked by other residents if they can join in. This could become the core of a small, regular communion service, and such provision is often appreciated by the home's staff.

Identity Shock and Isolation

We understand our identity as we relate to our environment, way of life and relationships. When moving into a home a great deal changes. People are totally and suddenly removed, or uprooted, from what is the norm—home, neighbours, and daily routine. They are removed from physical reminders of their past, their loved ones, and the memories that have been part of living where they were.

They are in a world of new faces, carers, smells, noises, and experiences. The world is likely to be clinically clean rather than shuffling round the piles of accumulated life at home. There may also be things worrying them about money, disposal of their house, clearing away of furniture and possessions, for which there is no room in the home. There is a sudden loss of privacy. All their medical, physical and emotional life is on display, and others cannot avoid overhearing highly personal conversations, or details given in conversations with carers, social workers, or ministers. All this can be very difficult for them. People may not talk in terms of their identity—but in the space of a few hours their environment, way of life, and relationships have all changed. They are likely to feel that they do not belong to this new world, and are cut off from the world to which they do belong.

Passivity

This is a difficult thing for many to come to terms with. In the home many things are done *for* the residents, or *to* them—everything from being dressed to being washed or having their hair combed the 'wrong way'! And this is done to the resident when convenient to the carers, in their time and their way, rather than how it used to be done when living at home.

Affirmation and Continuity

Someone from the local church can be a valuable lifeline in this new world. We know their home, their family, the events of the past years. We can talk to them about a whole range of familiar things, so the continuity of their life is affirmed, making the transmission a little less traumatic. We can talk to them about things happening in the church, or give news that will interest them, or we can read to them something they enjoy, and so on.

7
Frequently Asked Questions

i) Can I Receive Communion with the Person I am Visiting?

If taking communion directly from a church service, you may receive communion during the main service, and again with the communicant you are visiting—if you so wish. Or you can wait to receive until your home-visit. On other occasions, you may choose whether or not to take communion. You are not required to do so.

ii) What Should I do if Interrupted During the Service?

It is helpful to ask the communicant if anyone is likely to call during the service—for example scheduled visits by a district nurse or meals on wheels, which are of uncertain timing. If the door bell goes and the communicant is disabled it may set an alarm process going if the door is not answered. Suggesting that they continue in quiet prayer while you answer the door can protect the integrity of the service. The caller can be invited to join you or asked to call back later. Do not invite someone in to wait in another room—issues of security are extremely important here. Interruptions from communicants having breathing problems, a coughing fit, or being in extreme pain, are best dealt with by sympathetically waiting until they are ready to continue.

iii) What Do I Do if Someone Cannot Swallow the Bread?

If someone is very ill they may not be able to chew or swallow the bread. Only a very small piece should be used in the first place if this is likely. If it is spat out then take it in the purificator or tissue and dispose of it reverently as you would any consecrated bread.

iv) Should I Continue if the Communicant Falls Asleep or Unconscious?

A very old or very ill person may slip in and out of sleep or consciousness. If this happens frequently and only for short moments you can pause and continue when possible. Using the pauses to pray for the person is a good way of maintaining the integrity of the service and using the time. If falling asleep is the only problem a gentle word of encouragement to wake up is appropriate. But sometimes it is necessary to leave the service until a time when the communicant is better able to participate.

It is thought that those who are apparently unconscious may hear everything that is going on around them, as may someone drifting into sleep. So if a service does need to be ended, it is a good idea to pray for the person (perhaps with the laying on of hands) and close with the Lord's Prayer, which is familiar and may be echoed internally, and a prayer of blessing.

8
Training

Taking communion is a privilege, and a ministry which brings us close to the most personal area of someone's life. It is both humbling and inspiring to share someone's spiritual journey, and help them to relate to God in their situation. Appropriate training will help the minister prepare as they become aware of the responsibility of their call. It will also help the communicant, by ensuring competent ministry. Knowing that a communion minister has received some training and authorization enables the communicant to have some measure of confidence and trust in the one coming to them. As this may involve issues of confidentiality this is very important.

In some dioceses the training is centralized and authorization of a lay person to distribute Holy Communion can only be given to those who have attended.

A Sample Training Course
This could run over two days, or as an evening course over six weeks. Its aim is to prepare for their ministry those who will be authorized to distribute Holy Communion to church members absent from a celebration, in particular the sick and housebound. Its objectives are to ensure an understanding of the service of Holy Communion, to recognize the spiritual dynamic of a Holy Communion service, to raise awareness of the pastoral issues involved in ministering to the sick or housebound in their own home, or in a residential home, and to build a supportive team of those involved in this ministry.

Session 1: What Communion means
What Communion means to me—plenary brain-storm
A review of the biblical background of Holy Communion—Bible Study on the Passover, the Last Supper, the Corinthian church. Discussion on what the Scriptures tell us about this service.
What are we doing when giving communion in a home—discussion of the nature of the Body of Christ.

Session 2: What is happening during Communion?
Meeting with God—teaching on the theology of the Holy Communion. Discussion about the spiritual aspects and pastoral implications of these.
The dynamic of the service—using the usual form of Sunday service: in small groups, identify the 'conversation' that is taking place with God through the service; in plenary, mark out the structure of the service. Discuss the rationale and flow of the service.

Session 3: Setting the scene

What it is like to be ill at home and to be housebound—hearing two stories, by tape or in person.

Discussion of implications for home communion—group work in two groups (one on each of above). Plenary feed-back from groups.

Do's and Don'ts in home communions—drawing up a prioritized list from above feed-back.

Session 4: Who can minister in a Home Communion?

Who can minister? Information on the technicalities of who can minister.

Dealing with concerns—two statements: what most concerns me; what I most look forward to. Write down answers individually; discuss in pairs; discuss in plenary.

Praying together—discussion on the aims and form of prayer for those at home: confession; intercession; laying on of hands; anointing.

Issues of confidentiality—short talk and discussion on this important issue.

Session 5: How to minister in a Home Communion

Practical Session—setting up the room and the communion table; demonstration in role play; go through the service in pairs.

Feed-back and discussion in plenary.

Resources available—introduction to materials: books of readings; books of prayers; ideas for sharing news.

Home-work (this will need to be done after Session 3 if the course is done over 2 days)—go through the service with someone at home, as if taking them communion. Draw up a list of any questions that need addressing.

Session 6: Preparing to go

Preparation

Plenary brain-storm: What must I do to be ready? Go through what needs to be done, with a hand-out or this booklet.

Setting out—explain the procedure for leaving the service: prayer, receiving the elements, practicalities. Explain the procedure for using bread and wine kept in a safe place for this purpose.

Arriving and leaving—discussion of pastoral and practical considerations to remember.

Question Time—picking up any remaining questions from the home-run set as 'homework' or from the rest of the course.

Holy Communion and Prayer together—a short service, similar to that which will be used in the home, incorporating prayer for those who will minister and for those who will receive their ministry.